GRAND TETON
NATIONAL PARK

THE TETONS:
Children of The Rockies
by
George B. Robinson

SIERRA PRESS
MARIPOSA, CA

DEDICATION

This book is for my publisher Jeff Nicholas and my editor Nicky Leach. I will always think of them as more than publishing professionals. They are good friends, who share my passion for words and writing, and an irrepressible sense of wonder about the natural world. They have had unqualified faith in my ability and I have learned much from them. Their counsel has made my writing better.   —G.B.R.

ACKNOWLEDGMENTS

The author gratefully acknowledges the careful review and fact checking by Grand Teton National Park Chief of Interpretation Carolyn Richard, and Grand Teton Natural History Association Executive Director Jan Lynch and their respective staffs. Special thanks go to Jan Lynch who was a strong proponent of this publication. Having seen the author's book on Yellowstone in this series, she asked, "Why don't *we* have one?"   —G.B.R.

INSIDE FRONT COVER
Herd of bison moving across Antelope Flats.
PHOTO ©JOSHUA HENSON/IDAHO STOCK MAGES

PAGE 2
The Tetons reflected in pool near Schwabacher Road.
PHOTO ©CARR CLIFTON

TITLE PAGE
Trumpeter swan and cygnets.
PHOTO ©DIANA STRATTON

PAGE 4 (BELOW)
Bison below Grand Teton.
PHOTO ©MARK WEBER/IDAHO STOCK IMAGES

PAGE 4/5
Dramatic sunset seen from Snake River Overlook.
PHOTO ©STEVE MOHLENKAMP

CONTENTS

PAGE 6/7
Bouquet of balsamroot in a summer meadow.
PHOTO ©PAT O'HARA
PAGE 7 (BELOW)
Great gray owl chick.
PHOTO ©DIANA STRATTON

THE SETTING

The Tetons at sunset from near Triangle X Ranch. PHOTO ©ALAN MAJCHROWICZ

No matter how tightly the body may be chained
to the wheel of daily duties, the spirit is free . . .
to bear itself away from noise and vexation
into the secret places of the mountains.
— *At the North of Bearcamp Water*
Frank Bolles

I first saw the Teton Range nearly 60 years ago. I was with my father (who was stationed in the National Park Service Midwest Regional Office in Omaha) on an annual inspection tour of parks in the Central and Northern Rockies in the early 1950s. We were driving west over Togwotee Pass in the Wind River Range when Dad said, "There they are, son!"

The serrated peaks of the Tetons dominated the distant view. I had seen them recently in the movie *Shane*, but only as a scenic backdrop to the action on screen. These mountains were real, not celluloid images, and their mirrored reflection in Jackson Lake, as we approached Moran Junction, made them appear even more impressive, seeming to rise higher out of the valley floor as I watched.

I had seen and lived in mountains before but their contours had been less severe. These peaks looked more like what I imagined the Swiss Alps to be. That early impression of Jackson Hole, buttressed on the west by the massive Tetons, remains vivid in my memory. It augured a time—long in the future—when I would live and work in nearby Yellowstone National Park and often revisit the scene. I know of no other place that rivals the pure beauty of Jackson Hole and the incredible peaks abruptly rising above it.

Mountain men referred to enclosed mountain valleys, such as the one surrounding Jackson Lake, as "holes." Jackson Hole is a flat, upland valley consisting of porous, cobbled soils covered with sagebrush and surrounded by mountains and highlands. Jackson Hole, one of the largest such valleys in the Rocky Mountains, was named for David E. Jackson, a trapper who loved the Snake River country and, between 1824 and 1830, trapped along the Continental Divide. As a partner with Jedediah Smith and William Sublette, he kept their company financially stable through his competent trapping abilities and adept leadership.

Grand Teton National Park is small, yet it contains all of the classic elements associated with national parks of the West: mountains, abundant and diverse wildlife, pristine streams, rivers and glacial lakes, and different plant communities associated with changing elevations and microclimates. The spectacular vertical rise of the Tetons forms an abrupt contrast with the nearly flat sage-covered valley more than 7,000 feet below. Twelve Teton peaks reach above 12,000 feet and are high enough to support as many as 12 glaciers.

Grand Teton National Park and the John D. Rockefeller, Jr. Memorial Parkway total 333,700 acres within the Greater Yellowstone Ecosystem, more than 28,000 square miles of one of the few remaining, nearly intact, temperate zone ecosystems on the planet. Elevations range from 6,400 feet on the valley floor to 13,770 feet on the windswept granite summit of Grand Teton.

The Tetons are a textbook example of what geologists call fault-block mountains. The opposing blocks of rock forming the Tetons and Jackson Hole move along the Teton Fault, a major rift in the earth's surface along which movement may average about one vertical foot every 300 to 400 years. The range is about 40 miles long and 10 miles wide. It extends from Teton Pass on the south to the Berry Creek area near Yellowstone National Park. While the mountains rise abruptly on their eastern front, they slope more

OPPOSITE: Mount Moran reflected in the still waters of Oxbow Bend, autumn morning. PHOTO ©LARRY ULRICH

Historic Moulton Barn on Mormon Row, spring morning.

gently west into the Teton Basin in Idaho. Strangely, although the Tetons are the youngest mountains of the Rocky Mountain cordillera, they contain some of its oldest rocks, dating back about 2.5 billion years.

Sixty-one species of mammals, more than 300 species of birds, and at least 1,000 species of vascular plants are found in the park's four major habitats: the alpine zone, coniferous forests, sagebrush flats, and wetlands.

Grand Teton's archeological resources include 350 prehistoric sites, evidence of repeated use of both lowland and mountain areas by native peoples from about 11,000 to 300 years ago. More than 320 historic structures in the park, some with associated cultural landscapes, are listed in or eligible for listing in the National Register of Historic Places.

In an ecological sense, Grand Teton and Yellowstone national parks are inseparable parts of a much larger natural system. Lines drawn on maps define human boundaries, to indicate ownership, a territorial imperative that is foreign in the wild world. Those boundaries are mostly rectilinear and enclose legally defined entities. But natural boundaries are drawn by the resources themselves, such as rivers and mountain ranges. Most of the plants and animals that are characteristic of Yellowstone National Park are found in Grand Teton, too. And while they may act on a smaller stage, the ecological mechanisms are the same.

Each time I visit the Tetons, I am reminded that this is what primitive wild America was like. I watch a herd of bison along the Snake River, see a black bear in the distance skirting Emma Matilda Lake, or observe a few hundred elk grazing near Moose Junction. I imagine their numbers multiplied thousands of times. There were that many of these creatures ranging freely across North America when it was known only to indigenous peoples. As beautiful and impressive as these scenes are, they are a sad reminder for me of what we have lost in our progress from wilderness pioneers to citizens of an advanced and powerful nation. As available living space has dwindled, places like Grand Teton have become last refuges for many wild plants and animals.

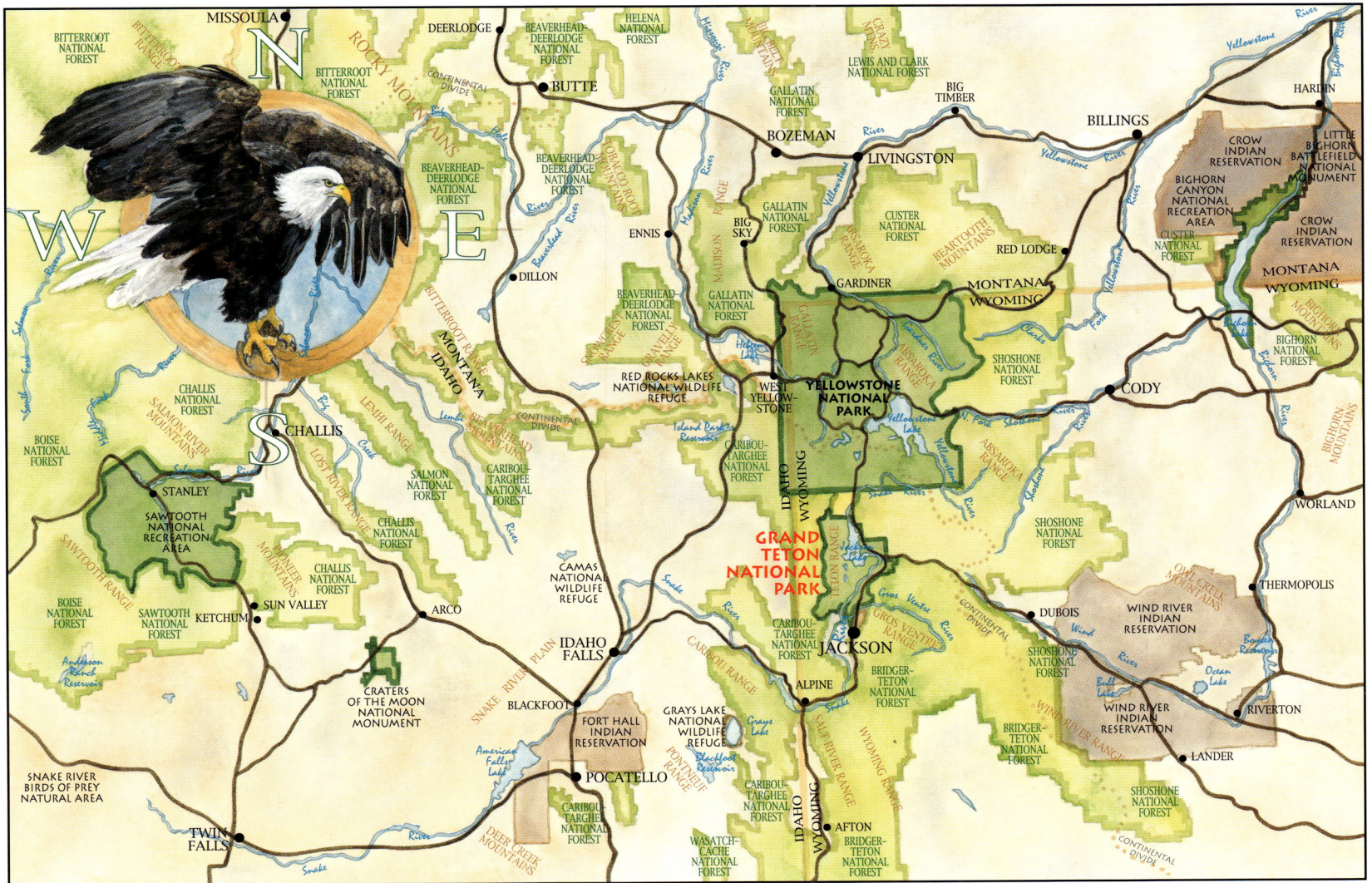

ILLUSTRATION BY DARLECE CLEVELAND

The Teton Range and Jackson Hole, located in northwest Wyoming, are part of the Rocky Mountain cordillera, the great chain of peaks that forms the backbone of North America from Alaska to Mexico, directing surface water flow to either the Atlantic or Pacific oceans. The cordillera is subdivided into three physiographic units: the Southern, Middle, and Northern Rockies. The Teton Range and Jackson Hole are in the Middle Rocky Mountains, an area comprised of smaller yet spectacular ranges imbedded among intervening semi-arid basins. The Jackson Hole area, in turn, divides two further physiographic areas: the Wyoming Basin to the southeast and the Columbia River Plateau to the west. The region is very different from most of the remainder of Wyoming, much of which lies largely in the Great Plains physiographic province.

From Jackson Hole and Grand Teton National Park, all of the cardinal points lead to a diverse array of scenic and historic attractions.

The world class Museum of the Rockies is on the campus of Montana State University in Bozeman, Montana is home to world-renowned paleontologist Jack Horner. Farther north, near Missoula, Montana, lies the Bob Marshall Wilderness. A huge escarpment known as the "Chinese Wall," averaging 1,000 feet in height and extending 22 miles along the Continental Divide, highlights its vast beauty. Missoula is the gateway to Glacier National Park and its sister Canadian park Waterton Lakes.

Cody, Wyoming, established by "Buffalo Bill" Cody, is the Eastern gateway to Yellowstone country. It is the home of the world class Draper Museum of Natural History, completed in 2002, and focusing entirely on the human and natural history of the Greater Yellowstone region. The sce-nic Bighorn Mountains, Bighorn Canyon National Recreation Area, and Little Bighorn Battlefield National Monument are east of Cody.

Not far south of Jackson lies Gannett Peak, at 13,804 feet, it is the highest point in Wyoming. Fossil Butte National Monument and Flaming Gorge National Recreation Area are some distance farther south of Jackson Hole.

West of Jackson Hole, in Idaho, is Hagerman Fossil Beds National Monument which protects the largest concentration of Hagerman Horse fossils in North America. Craters of the Moon National Monument is one of the best places in the world to see the effects of volcanism. The monument is a few miles north of the spectacular Twin Falls of the Snake River, and east of the Sawtooth National Recreation Area.

PAGE 12/13: The Tetons rise above the seasonally low waters of the Snake River, summer.
PHOTO ©ALAN MAJCHROWICZ

The Geologic Story

Aerial view of the Tetons at sunset from the west side. PHOTO ©TOM TILL

The major geologic processes that shaped the overall landscape of Jackson Hole and the Tetons were mountain building—a process that geologists call orogenesis—and glaciation. Other mountain ranges are formed by gradual uplift and folding of rock layers, such as the kind of volcanic activity manifested in Yellowstone and the Absaroka Range, or as a result of the collision of continental tectonic plates. But the Tetons are a classic fault-block mountain range, created by the opposing vertical movement of blocks of rock in the earth's crust. They rise along the Teton Fault, a rift, or break, that extends along the base of the entire length of the Teton Range's eastern front. On the east side of the Teton Fault, another block of the earth's crust—the valley of Jackson Hole—dropped as the mountains rose.

The Tetons are six to 10 million years old, just a few seconds on the clock of geologic time. They are the youngest and perhaps most spectacular mountain range in the Great Divide—the children of the Rockies. In contrast, the larger body of the Rocky Mountains is 50 to 60 million years old. Oddly, the youthful Teton Mountains contain some of the oldest rocks on the planet—basement rocks that began to form more than 2.5 billion years ago.

These parent rocks began to form when sand and volcanic debris settled in an ancient ocean. Sediment continued to accumulate to great depths for millions of years, and heat and pressure generated by the overlying layers eventually changed the sediment into a metamorphic rock called gneiss, the rock that comprises the main mass of the Teton Range. During metamorphosis, minerals separated out in the rock and formed distinctive patterns. Alternating light and dark layers identify banded gneiss, which can be seen in Death Canyon and in other canyons in the Teton Range.

Later in geologic time, molten rock forced its way up through cracks and zones of weakness in the gneiss. This igneous, or volcanic, rock slowly cooled, forming light-colored intrusions (dikes) of granite, inches to hundreds of feet thick, some of which can be seen from vantage points near Jenny Lake and String Lake. Uplift and erosion—the slow, steady work of weathering, particularly wind and moving water—have exposed the granite that now forms the main part of the range.

Diabase, a dark-colored igneous rock, forced its way up through the gneiss and granite, forming the prominent vertical dikes on the faces of Mount Moran and Middle Teton about 1.3 billion years ago. The diabase dike on Mount Moran protrudes from the face because the gneiss surrounding it erodes faster than the diabase, a process known as differential erosion. On the other hand, the diabase dike on Middle Teton is recessed because the granite of the central peaks erodes more slowly than the diabase.

The shallow seas that covered, retreated from, and advanced over the Teton region 600 million to 65 million years ago left sedimentary formations, still visible at the north and south ends of the Teton Range and also on the west slope of the mountains. Tiny trilobites, corals, brachiopods and other primitive marine organisms flourished in this marine environment. Their fossilized remains are preserved in the younger sedimentary rocks. As the more recent seas retreated, the area became a low-lying coastal plain frequented by dinosaurs. Fossilized bones of a horned dinosaur, the Triceratops, have been found east of the park near Togwotee Pass.

Compression of the earth's crust 80 million to 40 million years ago, resulting from the collision of the North American and Pacific tectonic plates, caused uplift of the Rocky Mountain chain from what is now Mexico to Canada—a period of mountain building called the Laramide Orogeny. About six to 10 million years ago, with displacement along the Teton fault, the birth of the range and valley began. The adjoining blocks moved vertically in opposite directions resulting in one fault block jutting upward, while the other block dropped

Detail view of banded gneiss. PHOTO ©JEFF FOOTT

Cobbled bottom of Jenny Lake and the Cathedral Group. PHOTO ©ED CALLAERT

abruptly, forming the valley floor.

Total vertical displacement along this fault has been close to 23,000 feet. The valley of Jackson Hole dropped 16,000 feet, more than twice as much as the mountains rose. The amount of displacement is demonstrated by the location of the Flathead Sandstone. Activity along the Teton fault separated this formation on the opposing blocks. On the summit of Mount Moran, 6,000 feet above the valley floor, lies a pink cap of Flathead Sandstone, visible when the snow has melted. On the valley side of the fault, this formation lies buried at least 24,000 feet below the surface.

Among the deposits filling Jackson Hole are some containing a large number of rounded rocks, varying in color from white to pink and purple. Ancient rivers carried the rocks here from an ancestral mountain range, 20 to 70 miles northwest of the Tetons. Tumbled in the rivers, the quartzite was rounded into cobblestones as it was carried into this area.

Massive volcanic activity took place in the west and north, beginning more than 20 million years ago, a series of events that covered the entire region in volcanic ash. More volcanic ash accumulated on the sinking floor of Jackson Hole nine to 10 million years ago, reaching a depth of nearly one mile. Between 600,000 and 6,000 years ago, incandescent clouds of gaseous molten rock issued from the collapse of a giant caldera in what is now central Yellowstone National Park and flowed southward on both sides of the Teton Range. Remnants of this pyroclastic flow are exposed on Signal Mountain and on the north end of the Teton Range.

In relatively recent geologic time, repeated glaciations resurfaced the topography of the Jackson Hole region. Glaciers move down slopes by their own weight, like giant icy rasps. Ten different glaciations have occurred in Jackson Hole over the last million years. Only two have left significant evidence of their passage. The older of the two, the Munger Glaciation, advanced into the valley 140,000 to 160,000 years ago. During this period, a massive glacier filled Jackson Hole with ice up to 4,000 feet thick. The more recent Pinedale Glaciation, which occurred in three phases, began 40,000 to 70,000 years ago and ended 12,000 to 15,000 years ago.

The glaciers' handiwork is apparent in the mountains and valleys today. Glaciers carved deep, U-shaped valleys and natural amphitheaters at the heads of canyons called cirques. Tarns, sapphire-colored lakes, often form in these bowl-like basins. Several small, thousand-year-old reentrant glaciers, reminders of an earlier frigid time, still cling to remote shaded recesses in the Tetons.

As they moved, Teton's glaciers picked up substantial loads of rocks and other debris, which was deposited as prominent terminal and lateral moraines that form the basins and sides of the spectacular piedmont lakes—Jenny, Leigh, Bradley, Taggart, Phelps—along the base of the range. Glaciers in the valley created other prominent moraines, such as Burned Ridge and Timbered Island. The appearance of these forested ridges is different from the surrounding sagebrush flats, indicating that moraine soils have a different composition. The Potholes, a sage-covered area pitted with many large craterlike depressions, is an area northeast of Burned Ridge. These depressions were formed by large pieces of ice that were buried under the soil as the glaciers receded. Known as kettles, they reappeared as the ice melted slowly over time. The sagebrush plant community dominates glacial outwash plains formed by millions of quartzite cobbles carried here from other nearby mountain ranges by water from melting glaciers.

Although the last great ice sheets melted about 15,000 years ago, a dozen small glaciers still exist in the Teton Range. They are reminders that water in all of its forms is a powerful geologic force.

The Human Story

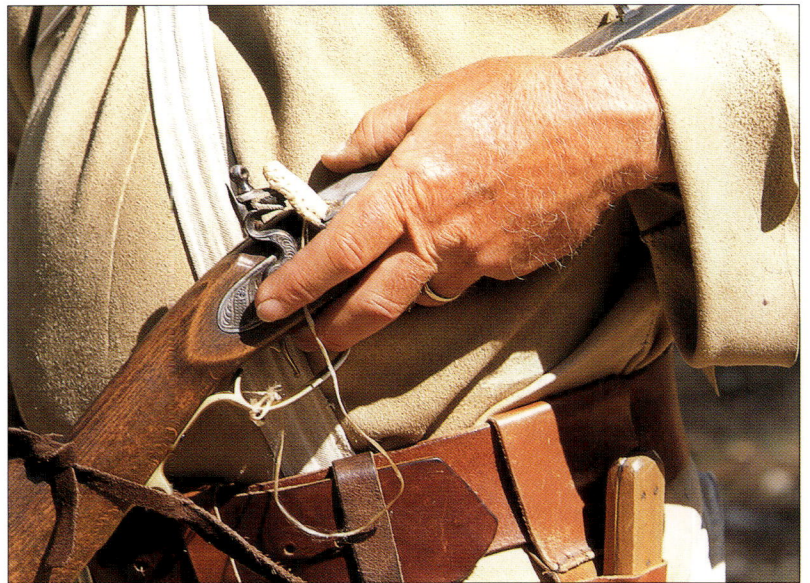

Mountain man wardrobe as worn by a period reenactor. PHOTO ©CAROL POLICH

People have a long association with Jackson Hole, Grand Teton, and the Greater Yellowstone area. The first humans to enter the region likely were ice-age immigrants who had crossed the Bering Land Bridge. They probably arrived sometime before 12,000 years ago. They may have been nomadic big-game hunters following large mammals into the region. These primitive hunters sought now-extinct animals such as wooly mammoths, giant sloths, and camels, but also pursued species that are common today, such as bison, elk, deer, bighorn sheep, and bears.

As the climate slowly warmed and dried, these new residents slowly adapted to the changing conditions of their environment and to the disappearance of some of their game. By about 7,000 years ago, the larger animals had become scarce and disappeared, so early hunters could not rely on them as prey. Instead, smaller game such as deer and bighorn sheep became important in their diet, along with plants such as bitterroot and pricklypear.

Archaeologists have found little physical evidence of Paleo-Indian presence other than their distinctive stone tools and projectile points. These lithic remnants, however, present a clear record of early human presence in the area over a long period. They include projectile points and flaky debris from their manufacture; evidence of the quarrying and widespread distribution of volcanic glass or obsidian—probably obtained from Yellowstone—for arrow and spear points; and habitation sites.

During the 1930s, a Jackson Hole rancher named W. C. Lawrence began to collect artifacts along the north side of Jackson Lake. For 30 years, Lawrence's collection grew to number in the thousands and helped confirm thousands of years of human habitation in Jackson Hole and Grand Teton National Park.

The earliest artifacts made by human hands in Jackson Hole date from between 12,000 and 8,000 years ago. During this time, the archeological record suggests that humans hunted with finely flaked, lanceolate-shaped, stone spear points. These points were hafted to a large spear that was either hand-thrown or projected by the use of an atlatl, a primitive yet effective spear thrower.

In general, the archeological record reveals little cultural change in the period between 12,000 and 500 years ago. The primary meat sources for mountain-dwelling humans were deer, elk, bighorn sheep, and some bison—while bison and antelope were staples for residents of the Great Plains.

Members of several modern American Indian tribes are known to have entered Jackson Hole during the past several hundred years, especially after they acquired the horse. Among the tribes that have connections with the area are the Blackfoot, Crow, Shoshone, Gros Ventre, and Bannock. In addition to evidence such as tipi rings and wickiups, their presence is documented in the journals of early mountain men and explorers such as Jim Bridger, Osborne Russell, Joe Meek, and others.

The Shoshone referred to individual tribal bands by the principal food of the group. Thus, within the larger tribe there were Buffalo Eaters, Salmon Eaters, Rabbit Eaters, and Sheepeaters. The Sheepeaters were the only long-term Indian residents in the area.

In 1803, President Thomas Jefferson organized the Lewis and Clark Corps of Discovery expedition to explore the unknown territory of the Louisiana Purchase. Setting out in May 1804 from Camp Wood, Missouri, the 25-member expedition traveled up the Missouri River and crossed the Rocky Mountains in Montana en route to the Pacific Ocean. John Colter, one of the members of the expedition, headed back into the mountains to scout for a fur-trading company during the return journey, in 1806. On a trip to the Crow country, Colter probably entered Jackson Hole in the winter of 1807-8. He traveled into Crow territory to persuade them to trap for valuable beaver pelts, which were used for the fashionable hats of the era.

Most of the famous mountain men that trapped in the West in the early 1800s traveled the trails that crossed the valley. Certainly, Jim

Historic Cunningham Cabin, early morning. PHOTO ©MARY LIZ AUSTIN

The Grand Teton seen through a window on Mormon Row. PHOTO ©GEORGE WUERTHNER

Bridger, Jedediah Smith, and William Sublette were among them. They traveled through the area, going to and from the annual summer rendezvous at Pierre's Hole, Idaho; Burnt Fork, Wyoming; and other sites, where they traded their beaver pelts and celebrated a successful trapping season.

From 1810 to 1840, Jackson Hole formed the crossroads of the six main trapper trails that traversed the region. From 1824 to 1840, mountain men came down from the mountains to sell their furs or trade for winter supplies with companies like the powerful Hudson's Bay Company and the Astoria Fur Company. These gatherings also allowed the rugged trappers a chance to eat, drink, and share "tall tales" with other trappers, as well as test their ability in contests of skill. The valley became the hub of the fur trade in the northern Rockies. Trappers used the Tetons as major landmarks. In fact, it was lovelorn French-Canadian trappers who first gave the name Tetons, an affectionate name for breasts, to these mountains.

By 1845, the fur trade had ended, as the fashion for men's beaver hats back East gave way to silk hats. For the next four decades, Jackson Hole remained unsettled because of its relative isolation and reverted to being used as the summer habitation of various Indian tribes and an occasional government expedition.

The Hayden Surveys of 1871, 1872, and 1878 officially named many of the important landmarks. Leigh Lake and Jenny Lake were named in honor of the guide for the 1872 expedition, Richard "Beaver Dick" Leigh. Beaver Dick was one of the last of the mountain man trappers who lived in the valley. Jenny Lake was named for his wife, a Shoshone woman, and Leigh Lake was named for Beaver Dick himself.

A member of the Hayden Expedition of 1871 and 1872, William Henry Jackson, took the first photographs of the Teton Mountains and Yellowstone. Jackson's impressive photographs caused a stir back East and were instrumental in convincing the federal government to set aside and protect the Yellowstone area as the world's first national park in 1872. After the creation of Yellowstone, big-game hunters and the first "dudes," including foreign royalty, visited the area.

By the 1890s, the villages of Kelly, Wilson, and Moran had been born. In 1892, two years after Wyoming became a state, Bill Menor moved into Jackson Hole, the first settler west of the Snake River. He established a ferry that remained for many years the only dry way to get across the Snake River. His cabin, in what is now Grand Teton National Park, has been preserved to house artifacts of the early settlers in Jackson Hole.

Cattle ranching became the major focus in the area, and with cattle ranching came a larger and more permanent settlement. The town of Jackson was founded in 1894 and acquired a plan for streets and major buildings in 1900. Some of the buildings and houses of that early era remain a part of Jackson today.

Concern for wintering elk began early in Jackson Hole. The U.S. Biological Survey Elk Refuge was established in 1912 with an allotment of one thousand acres. Today, the National Elk Refuge, the successor to the original refuge, contains nearly 25,000 acres and feeds more than 7,000 elk every winter.

Grand Teton National Park was established in 1929; Jackson Hole National Monument was created in 1943. The two units were combined to become present-day Grand Teton National Park in 1950. John D. Rockefeller, Jr. Memorial Parkway was established in 1972 to commemorate the philanthropic activities of John D. Rockefeller, Jr. especially his generous donation of 52 square miles of land he had acquired in the 1930s and 1940s.

Grand Teton is in many ways emblematic of the entire National Park System. Located in the heart of the Greater Yellowstone Ecosystem, it focuses attention on myriad nationally significant conservation issues. These include grazing, brucellosis, winter use, open space, fire management, wolf restoration, and water and air quality monitoring.

A beaver pond, the mountain man's favorite sight, reflecting the Tetons, early morning.

MOUNTAIN MEN

Author and historian Francis Parkman said of the mountain men, "I defy the annals of chivalry to furnish the record of a life more wild and perilous than that of a Rocky Mountain trapper." The trappers were a solitary, rugged, self-sufficient breed, and among the first non-indigenous people to venture into the western wilderness.

While their rough appearance and lifestyle might belie it, many mountain men were passable writers. None were more colorfully descriptive than Osborne Russell. Russell wasn't as famous as Jim Bridger, John Colter, or Jedediah Smith, but he kept a journal that provides us with a glimpse into the everyday life of the mountain men and how they coped in the mid-1800s. Through his writings, we are able to glimpse what the greater Yellowstone country was like more than 150 years ago. Russell was a keen observer of the land and the life of the times. Untrained as a journalist, he was nonetheless a sensitive and articulate writer who painted vivid verbal images. His journals include some of the earliest descriptions of the fauna, including the gray wolf, as well as character sketches of the Shoshone and Crow Indians.

According to Russell, the equipment of the mountain man was sparse and well used, and he provides an apt description of a typical mountain man, perhaps a mirror of himself.

"A Trappers equipment in such cases is generally one Animal upon which is placed . . . riding Saddle and bridle a sack containing six Beaver traps a blanket with an extra pair of Moccasins his powder horn and bullet pouch with a belt to which is attached a butcher Knife a small wooden box containing bait for Beaver a Tobacco sack with a pipe and implements for making fire with sometimes a hatchet fastened to the Pommel of his saddle his personal dress is a flannel or cotton shirt (if he is fortunate to obtain one, if not Antelope skin answers the purpose of over and under shirt) a pair of leather breeches with Blanket or smoked Buffalo skin, leggings, a coat made of Blanket or Buffalo robe a hat or Cap of wool, Buffalo or Otter skin his hose are pieces of Blanket lapped round his feet which are covered with a pair of Moccasins made of Dressed Deer Elk or Buffaloe skins with his long hair falling loosely over his shoulders complete the uniform."

OPPOSITE: Aspens on the shore of Jackson Lake, autumn afternoon. PHOTO ©WILLARD CLAY
PAGE 20/21: Mount Moran and the Tetons, Jackson Lake, sunset. PHOTO ©DIANA STRATTON

Afoot in the Tetons

The Tetons seen from the Teton Crest Trail, late afternoon. PHOTO ©SCOTT T. SMITH

I have been fortunate to spend the greater part of my life living and working in some of the most beautiful, historically rich, wild, and biologically diverse national parks in the world. Yet, one can live in a place and not truly come to know it. Some places shout for attention; others speak in whispers. But all of them reveal their essence only to those who take time to venture away from roads and developed areas, into the heart of the parks.

It is there that serendipitous discoveries are made, where one can come to truly understand the meaning of wilderness, the connections among living creatures. Only in the backcountry, or at least away from the clamor of park roads and developments, can visitors access the "real" park, come upon the hidden and little-known places and hear the sounds of wild critters, the wind, a distant rockfall, the voice of a mountain stream. It is in these locations that a person can experience an epiphany, a sudden revelation of meaning.

I have been to such places. They have spoken to me of the diversity and complexity that gird the natural world, the abiding nature of ecological process, the connections among living things and the physical world, the inevitability of death, and the certainty of rebirth. My experiences in the backcountry have placed me in the proper context with wild things, and made it clear to me how parks are relevant to my life and times. It is when we are in the wild that we can, as writer Barry Lopez has said, "renegotiate our contracts with Nature."

For those who can take the time, are physically fit, and searching for more than a superficial park experience, there are 230 miles of trails forming an access network into the otherwise hidden places where the essence of Grand Teton lies. But a word of caution. Too often, we make haste to stay with an itinerary. Con-

centrating on the past or the future rather than the present moment, we see the form but fail to experience the essence. Often we are driven by the imperative of the designated scenic trail or route. They tell us that they alone lead to significant or especially scenic places, and that our experience will be incomplete if we don't to get to those destinations. In our myopic focus on the end of the trail, we can fail to make hundreds of intimate connections with Nature along the way.

Eastern philosophers believe that the laws of Nature and its processes follow Tao or The Way. They believe that all things have form and essence. Form is palpable. It is linear and can be seen, felt, weighed, and measured. Essence is energy and is infinite. It is nonlinear and cannot be touched, counted, or timed. Yet, it is essence that sustains and animates form. Form without essence is empty and lifeless; essence cannot be manifested without form. In all things there are complementary opposites: yin and yang, life and death, male and female, light and darkness, day and night, winter and summer, flood and drought, matter and spirit. At the heart of science is the act of measurement. Something may be beautiful, emotionally moving, intellectually meaningful, and relevant, but if it cannot be put on a scale or in a flask nor its length, width, and volume determined, it is of little interest to science. The essence of things can only be calculated in intangible personal terms, and must be experienced by the individual.

A cursory visit limited to park roads, visitor centers, and developed areas, and a focus on the icons that conventional wisdom identifies with the park, conspire to make one's experience less meaningful. True to Nature's economic protocols, small things are of value. Grand Teton is much more than majestic snow-capped mountains, moose, elk, and grizzly bears. It is slime molds,

OPPOSITE: Last light on Grand Teton and North Fork of Cascade Creek, summer. PHOTO ©ERIC WUNROW

Bluebells and geranium leaves in a meadow near Oxbow Bend.

lichens, boreal toads, army cutworm moths, big leaf sagebrush, caddisflies, and chipping sparrows, too. There are millions of small organisms dwelling at the foundation of the ecological structures of the park. The seldom seen, commonplace, and unheralded things are uncommonly important players in the living drama enacted daily on the geological stage in Grand Teton.

While afoot in the park, focus your binoculars not just on the summit of Grand Teton or Mount Moran, a bull moose browsing along the shore at Oxbow Bend, a 2000-pound bison near Signal Mountain, or a bald eagle soaring overhead. Move closer! Train your field glasses on a nearby anise swallowtail or a sagebrush lizard. Embark on a hand-lens adventure by examining a lichen-covered glacial erratic boulder, or the crystalline structure of an ancient piece of gneiss. You'll be well rewarded.

Close-up view of cracked and shattered ice, mid-winter. PHOTO ©DIANA STRATTON

Located in northwestern Wyoming, Grand Teton National Park and the John D. Rockefeller, Jr. Memorial Parkway preserve a spectacular landscape rich with majestic mountains, pristine lakes, and extraordinary wildlife.

A narrow scenic parkway connects Grand Teton and Yellowstone national parks. The late conservationist and philanthropist John D. Rockefeller, Jr. made significant contributions to several national parks, including Grand Teton, Acadia, Great Smoky Mountains, and Virgin Islands. In 1972, Congress dedicated the 24,000-acre parcel of land and the highway from the south boundary of Grand Teton to West Thumb in Yellowstone as John D. Rockefeller, Jr. Memorial Parkway to recognize his generosity and foresight.

There are approximately 100 miles of park roads, which are usually very congested during the summer season. Always consider driving time and distance to your next destination before setting out. Trail mileage in the park totals 230 miles. Most park trails are rough rock or dirt and are not accessible to visitors with disabilities. There are many asphalt trails in the Jenny Lake area, some of which are accessible. Some trails may begin as asphalt and change to dirt or gravel shortly thereafter.

There are three visitor centers in the park. They are located at Moose, Jenny Lake, and Colter Bay. An information station is located at Flagg Ranch on the John D. Rockefeller, Jr. Memorial Parkway. Only the Craig Thomas Discovery and Visitor Center at Moose is open year round, except for Christmas Day. In the summer of 2008, an additional visitor facility will open at the Laurance S. Rockefeller Preserve. It will provide visitors with an introduction to the old JY Ranch property. Park concessionaires operate hotels, restaurants, gift shops, service stations, stores, and marinas. It is a good

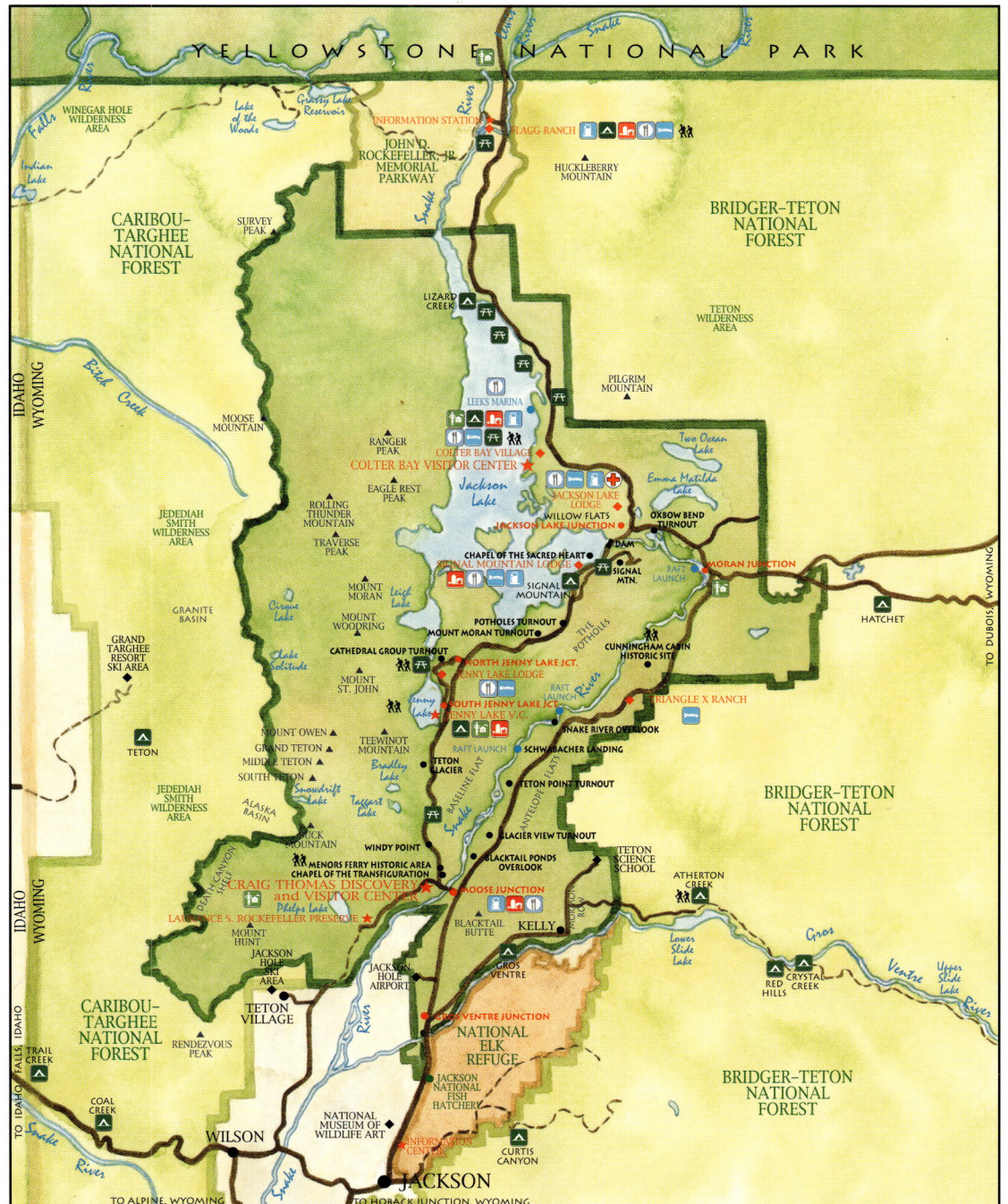

ILLUSTRATION BY DARLECE CLEVELAND

idea to make reservations well in advance of your visit—a year is not too early!

Campgrounds are located at Gros Ventre, Jenny Lake, Colter Bay, Lizard Creek, and Signal Mountain. Camping and RV sites at Flagg Ranch provide accessible facilities.

Most park roads are closed during the winter, but some are groomed for travel in snowmobiles. Check for information at visitor service desks in concession facilities, or at visitor centers. If you prefer to ski, several fine cross-country ski trails are maintained.

To learn more about Grand Teton, see the exhibits at visitor centers, or participate in interpretive programs, such as guided walks, campfire talks, demonstrations, and other activities available free of charge.

Seasons In The Wild

Aspens and conifers dusted with the season's first snowfall. PHOTO ©ELIZABETH BOEHM

Climate has a profound effect on the environment and the lives of plants and animals of Jackson Hole and Grand Teton. Snowfall covers the ground in the valley from November through April. Moose averages 23 inches of precipitation annually. During the winter, a mantle of snow 20 to 40 inches deep covers the valley floor. However, precipitation is extremely variable throughout the valley because of elevation and the rain shadow caused by the Teton Range.

In September, the leaves begin to fall from the aspens and cottonwoods in the valley, the air chills a bit, and the days grow shorter. Winter approaches rather quickly, and evening temperatures drop into the 20s or 30s° Fahrenheit. It's not long before they tumble to below zero. In the chilled morning air, frost covers the ground and vegetation, and occasional snow flurries dust the valley floor. Higher up, clouds conceal the heavier snow they are dropping on the Tetons. It is time to prepare for the typically long, cold, and demanding winter. I can don boots and a down vest, move inside, and seek the scented warmth of a fireplace, but how do my wild brethren cope with the changing conditions

Bears, Uinta and golden-mantled ground squirrels, yellow-bellied marmots, least chipmunks, and some other mammals weather the long winters by entering winter sleep or hibernating. Both processes involve greatly reduced metabolic activity and lowered body temperature. The hibernators and sleepers feed heavily during the fall, bulking up with fat reserves.

Bears enter dens as winter approaches, and fall into winter sleep, but their body temperature, normally about 100°F, only drops a few degrees, and seldom gets below about 88°F. Bears are not true hibernators. During winter sleep, they are warm and capable of activity, and females give birth and suckle their cubs. Unlike true hibernators, whose body temperatures are quite low, bears can respond to external stimulation and sometimes wake up and leave their dens during winter.

True hibernators, such as ground squirrels, enter protected burrows underground and build nests of grass and other materials. Here, they curl up in a ball, with their extremities tucked tightly against the body to reduce surface-to-volume ratio. When the animal's body temperature has nearly reached the outside temperature, it appears to be dead: its respiration is imperceptible; it does not react to outside stimuli; nor does it react to being handled and uncurled. Changes in the circulatory system allow the brain temperature of hibernators to remain a few degrees warmer than the environmental level. This enables the temperature of the brain to remain constant despite fluctuations in the temperature of the skin. Certain nervous pathways are maintained to regulate and coordinate metabolism as temperatures drop. This adaptation of the nervous system enables changes in the environment to be perceived, even when the animal is torpid. During hibernation as much as 40 percent of the total body weight may be lost.

Deer mice huddle together to stay warm. The northern pocket gopher and other small mammals live under the snow, where they are insulated and safe from predators. In the spring, after snow has melted, the winter work of the pocket gopher is evident. Gopher cores, long serpentine coils of earth left behind as the gopher burrowed under the snow, remain. Northern flying squirrels keep warm in nests of shredded bark in abandoned woodpecker holes in snags. They feed on nuts and seeds that they have stored at the base of trees. Red squirrels and beavers store, or cache, food before winter. Pikas harvest stems and leaves of various small shrubs, grasses, and weeds and lay them out to dry in built "haystacks" among the rocks. These reserves provide food for pikas through long winters.

OPPOSITE: Late afternoon at Snake River Overlook, autumn. PHOTO ©LARRY ULRICH

PAGE 28/29: Dramatic dawn light striking Grand Teton, mid winter. PHOTO ©CAROL POLICH

Moose and Mount Moran. PHOTO ©DIANA STRATTON

Family of river otters. PHOTO ©DIANA STRATTON

Coyote listening attentively for prey beneath the snow. PHOTO ©GEORGE ROBBINS

Mammals (other than humans) molt, or shed, their fur in fall. Longer guard hairs, the characteristics of which vary with species, are sometimes hollow or colorless, and contain insulating trapped air that protects the underfur. River otters, for example, have dense underfur. It is protected by long guard hairs with interlocking spikes that trap insulating air. Oil secreted from sebaceous glands waterproofs the fur so that no water reaches the skin. Otters dry themselves and restore air to their fur by rolling in the snow and vigorously shaking just like domestic dogs. Mammals also can fluff their fur up to trap air when they are cold and flatten it down to remove air when they are warm.

Snowshoe hares and weasels exchange their dark coats for white in winter. White color is an adaptive camouflage, but it may be more important for winter survival as an insulator because hollow white hairs contain air instead of pigment. Snowshoe hares have large feet to spread their weight over the snow; martens and lynx grow additional fur between their toes, which makes it easier for them to walk on snow.

Wild ungulates adapt to the onset of winter by migrating vertically downward. Elk and deer move to lower valleys. Bison, elk, and deer sometimes save energy by walking in long lines through deep snow. In an adaptation to the winter activities of people, bison and elk often follow roadways that have been groomed for snowmobile users. Bison seek out the warmer conditions in thermal areas, too, and bighorn sheep move to lower elevations on the mountain slopes and in the Teton foothills. Moose have special joints that allow them to swing their legs over snow rather than push through snow as elk do. Bison have very large shoulder muscles that form the distinctive humps in their backs. Those muscles enable bison to swing their huge heads back and forth sweeping the often-heavy snow aside in search of food.

Mammals and waterfowl have a unique heat exchange system in their legs that enables them to stand in cold water: Cold temperatures cause surface blood vessels to constrict, diverting blood into deeper veins that lie close to arteries. The cooled blood returning from extremities is also warmed by arterial blood traveling towards the extremities, conserving precious heat and energy.

Chorus frogs tolerate freezing by becoming severely diabetic in response to cold temperatures and the formation of ice within their bodies. At this point the liver quickly converts glycogen to glucose, which enters the blood stream and serves as a form of natural antifreeze. Within eight hours, blood sugar rises 200 percent. When a frog's internal ice content reaches 60–65 percent, the frog's heart and breathing stop. Within one hour of thawing, the heart resumes beating.

Some birds roost with their heads tucked into their fluffed-up back feathers to prevent heat loss. Grouse roost overnight by burrowing into snow for insulation. Chickadees roost in small

First light of a winter dawn raking across Oxbow Bend.

cavities. For the small and delicate chickadee, a half-inch-thick layer of insulating feathers can keep it up to 100°F warmer than the ambient temperature. At night, chickadees undergo a type of controlled hypothermia. Their body temperature drops from 108°F to 88°F, which lessens the sharp gradient between the temperature of their bodies and the external temperature. This leads to a 23 percent decrease in the amount of fat burned each night.

Many bird species escape the rigors of winter altogether by migrating to warmer places. Known as neotropical migrants, these birds spend the summer season in the Greater Yellowstone Ecosystem and winter in the neotropics. The land birds and songbirds belonging to this group spend the winter in western Mexico. Most of the swallows, sparrows, warblers, and blackbirds leave for the winter. Among the other migrants are American white pelicans, northern harriers, and other hawks; American kestrels and peregrine falcons; redheads, canvasbacks, green-winged teals, mallards, and most other ducks; rufous hummingbirds; and American pipits.

Warm weather begins in the valley and gradually moves upslope. Snow level retreats up the mountain canyons throughout the summer, revealing the stone face of the Tetons. Melting snow is followed by a profusion of wildflowers, as if they had lain dormant under the carpet of snow. Eventually snow melts from areas above treeline, and dwarf alpine plants begin to flower during the short season.

Although they appear barren and lifeless, the high alpine reaches of the park support plants specially adapted to the harsh growing conditions found there. Wind, snow, lack of soil, increased ultraviolet radiation, rapid and dramatic shifts in temperature, and a short growing season all challenge the hardy plants that survive here. Most plants adapt by growing close to the ground in mats like the alpine forget-me-not.

The Snake River seen from Snake River Overlook, sunset.

THE SNAKE RIVER

The Snake River is the nation's fourth largest and tenth longest (1,056 miles) watercourse. Named for the Shoshone or Snake Indians, it gathers runoff from the Two Ocean Plateau in Yellowstone National Park and traces 42 miles through the southern part of Yellowstone National Park. Later, aptly named Pacific Creek joins the Snake River after it flows out of Jackson Lake in Grand Teton National Park, then continues south through Jackson Hole and past the town of Jackson. The volume of the Snake is exceeded only by the Columbia River, of which it is the main artery, and its watershed drains 108,000 square miles. The Columbia, freshened by water carried from Yellowstone and Grand Teton, eventually wends its way to the Pacific Ocean.

From its headwaters along the Continental Divide in Yellowstone National Park to its confluence with the Columbia River near Pasco, Washington, the Snake drops 9,500 vertical feet. At Hells Canyon, along the Idaho/Oregon border, the Snake carves the deepest gorge in North America.

In Grand Teton and Jackson Hole, the Snake River creates a rich riparian habitat that supports a great diversity of wildlife. This reach of the Snake is home to the only native cutthroat trout subspecies (Snake River finespotted cutthroat) in the inland West that still completely dominates its historic range. Still, habitat alterations, manipulations of water flow, and the introduction of nonnative species are believed to have led to declines in this species, which is sometimes called the Jackson Hole cutthroat trout.

The gradient of the Snake River through the Jackson Hole area is about 19 feet per mile. Some reaches of the Snake are braided, while multiple channels are more common; meandering patterns are characteristic of stretches with lower gradients and sediment inputs. Tributaries draining the mountains tend to have high velocities even during low flows. In flood, they transport large sediment loads and spread out into a network of side channels, eroding the banks, changing courses frequently, and reforming the channel bed during a single flood.

The streams within Grand Teton drain a recently glaciated and geologically unstable region, and they carry high sediment loads that add to the landscape. The highest rates of aggradation—a modification of the earth's surface in the direction of uniformity of grade by deposition—happen near the base of the mountains, where several streams have created alluvial fans as they enter Jackson Hole. The plant and animal life inhabiting the park have evolved to coexist with, and in some cases be dependent upon, this instability.

OPPOSITE: Rosy glow of dawn on the Tetons from near Schwabacher Road. PHOTO ©JEFF D. NICHOLAS

Scorched hills beneath Grand Teton, Mount Owen, and Teewinot Mountain from near Taggart Lake Trailhead.

PHOTO ©ERIC WUNROW

THE ROLE OF FIRE

Greater Yellowstone Ecosystem landscapes, such as those in Grand Teton, have long been shaped by fire. The natural history of fire in the park includes periodic large-scale conflagrations sweeping across the region.

Such wildfires occurred across much of the ecosystem in the 1700s. But that was prior to the arrival of European explorers, the designation of the park, and the pattern established by its early caretakers to battle all blazes, believing that fire suppression was good stewardship. Throughout much of the 20th century, park managers and visitors alike continued to view fire as a destructive force, one to be mastered, or at least tempered. By the 1940s, ecologists recognized that fire was a primary agent of change in many ecosystems, including the arid U.S Mountain West. In the 1950s and 1960s, national parks and forests began to experiment with controlled burns, and by the 1970s parks had instituted a natural fire management plan to allow the process of lightning-caused fire to continue influencing wildland succession.

Many of the plant species in the Greater Yellowstone Ecosystem are fire adapted. Some (not all) of the lodgepole pines that make up a large percentage of the greater ecosystem's extensive forests have cones that are serotinous (sealed by resin) until the intense heat of fire cracks the bonds and releases the seeds inside. Fires may stimulate regeneration of sagebrush, aspen, and willows, but interactions among these plants and fire are complicated by other influences, such as grazing levels and climate. Though above-ground parts of grasses and forbs are consumed by flames, the below-ground root systems typically remain unharmed. In fact, for a few years after a fire, these plants commonly increase in productivity.

For the above reasons, fire is inextricably linked to the health and diversity of the Grand Teton landscape. The fire-adapted ecosystem depends on periodic wildfires to return plant communities to earlier successional stages and provide a variety of food sources and habitat for wildlife. Fire creates rather than destroys habitat. It produces vegetative mosaics and biologically rich and diverse community edges.

Resource managers in national parks today use natural fires and prescribed burns as part of a comprehensive fire plan. Natural fire, prescribed fire, fire effects monitoring, and hazard fuel reduction help restore natural processes while providing for firefighter and public safety.

OPPOSITE: String Lake and Mount Moran, early morning. PHOTO ©TIM FITZHARRIS
PAGE 36/37: Mount Moran and clearing clouds, autumn morning.
PHOTO ©WILLARD CLAY

THE WILD SIDE

Limber pine (known as "The Patriarch") frames the Cathedral Group. PHOTO ©JEFF GNASS

The massive rock bastion of the Teton Range and the flat, cobbled valley more than a mile below are stunning. The streams, rivers, foothill lakes, snow, and small glaciers clinging to shaded mountain recesses are beautiful and icy cold. The limpid air is crisp and soothing to my lungs. The temperate midsummer sun is bright and warm. All of the primal elements are manifest here: earth, water, air, and fire. But although they are essential, they can never replace the diverse assemblage of plants and animals that breathe life into the physical world. I feel a connection with Teton's wild things. Like people, they have formed into communities that animate the Teton landscape.

The sagebrush community is the largest biotic community in the park and supports the most diverse flora. It is largely treeless because the coarse, rocky soil doesn't hold water well; nevertheless, 100 species of plants have been identified in this zone. In midsummer, wildflowers add color to the otherwise stark sagebrush steppe. Sedges and grasses dominate meadows at higher, drier elevations. They are usually found in depressions and often flood during the spring. A high water table characterizes the shrub-swamp community. Shrubs such as willow, buffaloberry, silverberry, and serviceberry are typical species and important food sources for birds and mammals. Animals typical of this community include Uinta ground squirrels, badgers, coyotes, northern sagebrush lizards, pronghorn, sage grouse, and Swainson's hawks.

The areas along creeks, rivers, and lakes are called riparian communities. They form about 10 percent of the park and host a large variety of water-dependent wildlife. Along watercourses, the dominant trees are water-loving cottonwood, blue spruce, and willow trees. The willow community is similar to the shrub-swamp—both growing in areas where the water table is high and

soil drainage poor. A good example of this habitat type is Willow Flats near Jackson Lake Dam. Aquatic plants, insects, fish, and a multitude of invertebrates thicken the water with life. Beaver, muskrat, moose, and other water-dependent mammals make their homes here, along with osprey, bald eagles, swans, and various ducks. Bald eagles and ospreys feed exclusively on fish in rivers and lakes, and water is essential for the beaver's survival. Moose are drawn to these areas because willow is a favorite food source and critical to their winter survival.

The aspen community lies between sagebrush and marshland areas, with white-barked aspen dominating the scene. Groves of aspen—which clone from single root sprouts—cluster on dry hillsides and relatively flat areas. Birds such as woodpeckers, owls, ruffed grouse, and bluebirds congregate in this community: deer and elk forage here on aspen bark and other plants.

Some parts of the valley floor and most of the lower mountainsides, where lodgepole pine trees are the dominant species, constitute the lodgepole pine community. Understory vegetation is sparse because lodgepole pine stands are tall and closely ranked and tend to block sun from reaching the ground. Animals that frequent this community include bears, squirrels, porcupine, elk, deer, mountain chickadees, white-crowned and chipping sparrows, dark-eyed juncos, and great gray owls.

At higher elevations, the forest gives way to the spruce-fir community. Subalpine fir, Engelmann spruce, white bark pine—the seeds of which are an important food source for grizzly bears—and other coniferous trees dominate the forest. Moose reside here year round, as do mule deer and the elusive mountain lion. Watch the branches for nuthatches, dusky grouse, chickadees, and flycatchers.

The area from the tree line to the summit of the Tetons

OPPOSITE: The Tetons and Snake River Plain seen from the sagebrush flats near Cunningham Cabin, autumn morning.
PHOTO ©TERRY DONNELLY

Grand Teton rises above the dramatic, glacially-carved Death Canyon, seen from Death Canyon Shelf.

forms the alpine community; an area of harsh conditions that make special demands on the few lifeforms that can thrive there. Very hardy plants and animals make their homes in this arid, windy region. Most temporary animal residents are forced down to lower elevations by winter snow, ice, and plummeting temperatures. Still, in summer, mats of colorful phlox, alpine forget-me-nots, moss campion, mountain avens, and lichens, add color to the otherwise bleak environment. Some plants devote 90 percent of their structure to the root system, where they store nutrients and energy to help them through poor growing periods. Their flowers are often large but other plant parts are small to save energy and reduce exposure to the rigors of the wind and cold. Most of the plants are slow-growing perennials. Animals that can be found at these high altitudes include yellow-bellied marmots, bighorn sheep, pikas, Clark's nutcrackers, rosy finches, white-crowned sparrows, water pipits, and golden eagles. Variations in temperature cause intense freeze-thaw activity. Water in rock fissures exerts pressures of 29,000 pounds per square inch when it freezes.

This is enough to expand and break the enclosing rock.

The diversity of plant communities explains the rich variety of wildlife in the Teton country. Today, 61 species of mammals, including the large animals that are avatars of wild North America, inhabit parklands year round or seasonally. Hundreds of bird species fill every avian niche. This is remarkable when one considers the impact of more than a century of settlement and development. For example, settlers, particularly cattlemen arriving in Jackson Hole after 1900, were responsible for exterminating the gray wolf, which is only now being returned to its rightful place in the ecosystem. There were no bison left in Jackson Hole when the first homesteaders came in 1884. Their return began in the 1940s, when a small herd of 15 bison was introduced at the now defunct Jackson Hole Wildlife Park. In 1968, the herd broke through the fences and has been allowed to range freely since then. Recently, the grizzly bear has returned to its historic ranges in Jackson Hole.

Grizzly bear sow and her yearling cubs.

BEARS

Bears are icons of wild America and have always played a central role in the Greater Yellowstone Ecosystem. In Grand Teton National Park, specifically, black bears are often seen; grizzlies, more common in Yellowstone, have been observed more frequently in Grand Teton in recent years.

Unfortunately, when bears become accustomed to eating human food and garbage, they often turn into aggressive, destructive intruders who must be killed if they become a threat to visitors. Park managers say that "a fed bear is a dead bear," but according to one bear management specialist, "The worst day in bear management is when you have to euthanize an animal."

Grand Teton National Park has begun an information campaign to educate park visitors and local residents about how to behave safely in bear country. Known as the "Be Bear Aware" program, it has been initiated to augment the park's efforts to conserve grizzly bears, black bears, and other park wildlife. Visitors requesting information prior to their trip, and upon arrival in the park, see "Be Bear Aware" cautionary signs and posters throughout the park with reminders of the proper way to observe and interact with wild bears.

Strategically placed posters remind backcountry users, including climbers, to never leave backpacks or food unattended. Hikers camping overnight in Grand Teton National Park are required to carry and properly use bear food storage canisters, suspending them from trees well away from their campsites. Feeding of any park wildlife is prohibited. It is not necessary for an animal's wellbeing, and may ultimately lead to the animal's demise. Posters remind everyone that they can help save a bear by practicing good "leave no trace" habits, including proper storage of things such as food, clothing, toilet articles, and other things that might attract bears.

Recently, Grand Teton staff began a major review of the park's bear management program. Goals include restoring and maintaining the natural behavior and distribution of bears, improving visitor understanding and appreciation of bears, and improving visitor and animal safety by minimizing human confrontations with bears. Visitors are urged to respect an animal's need for space by keeping a safe distance: 100 yards from bears and 25 yards from other wild animals.

FLORA AND FAUNA

Colorado columbines in the high country. PHOTO ©JEFF FOOTT

PLANT COMMUNITIES

Both the altitude and the latitude of Grand Teton, along with differences in temperature and precipitation, influence the kinds of plants that grow here. The composition of soils, moisture content, slope, and exposure to sunlight also affect plant cover. Conditions vary from high desert to arctic tundra. Because Grand Teton and Jackson Hole lie just below the 45th parallel, they are near the midpoint between the Equator and the North Pole. In addition, their elevation ranges from 6,350 at the south park boundary, to 13,770 feet on the summit of the Grand Teton. An increase of 6,000 feet in elevation is roughly equivalent to traveling 1,800 miles north into the Canadian Arctic without leaving the national park.

As populations of plants and animals interact with one another they form biological communities. The term biodiversity refers to the number of species and individual organisms in these communities and the complexity of their relationships. In Nature, diversity and complexity denote health. Research has shown that species-rich communities are able to recover faster from disturbances than species-poor communities, a fact well illustrated by the ecosystem's dramatic recovery from the epic fires of 1988. The plants of Grand Teton National Park have evolved into the following communities: forests, sagebrush flats, riparian corridors and wetlands, and alpine areas.

Plant succession is an orderly and predictable sequence of plant communities occupying a site following a disturbance. Depending on the extent of the disturbance, some species may survive; other species may be restored from nearby habitats; and, others may actually be released from a dormant condition by the disturbance. Each new disturbance within a landscape creates an opportunity for a new species to colonize that region. New species also alter the character of the community, creating conditions that favor even newer species. Such cyclic disturbances, such as fires and earthquakes, occur periodically in Nature, creating plant mosaics and endlessly changing the patterns in the vegetation quilt.

What starts out as naked rock is ultimately clothed in living vegetation, with plants giving way to other plants. The first to populate Teton's raw rocks are mosses and lichens, which secrete acids that gradually break down their rocky hosts. Moss and lichen are supplanted by grass and rooted shrubs. Tall, mature trees eventually overshadow and replace smaller, shade-intolerant ones. At every stage, individual plant species exhibit characteristics that allow them to adapt to the soil, moisture, nutrients, lighting, and other conditions of the site, factors that are influenced by climate, elevation, topography, latitude, and other conditions. The process begins with the earliest community, known as the pioneer community, and continues until little change in species composition occurs, a condition referred to as the climax community.

More than a thousand species of vascular plants grow in Grand Teton National Park and the surrounding area. Evergreens, such as whitebark pine, limber pine, subalpine fir, and Engelmann spruce, have a conical shape and waxy needles that allow them to shrug off snow and survive the cold windy slopes and alpine zone high up in the Tetons. Other evergreens, such as lodgepole pine, Douglas fir, and blue spruce, are more comfortable on the valley floor, while aspens, cottonwoods, alders, and willows prefer the moist soils found along the rivers and lakeshores.

Where two biological communities adjoin they form what is called an ecotone, a zone where species from each community

Sunrise in the high country. PHOTO ©JOHN DITTLI

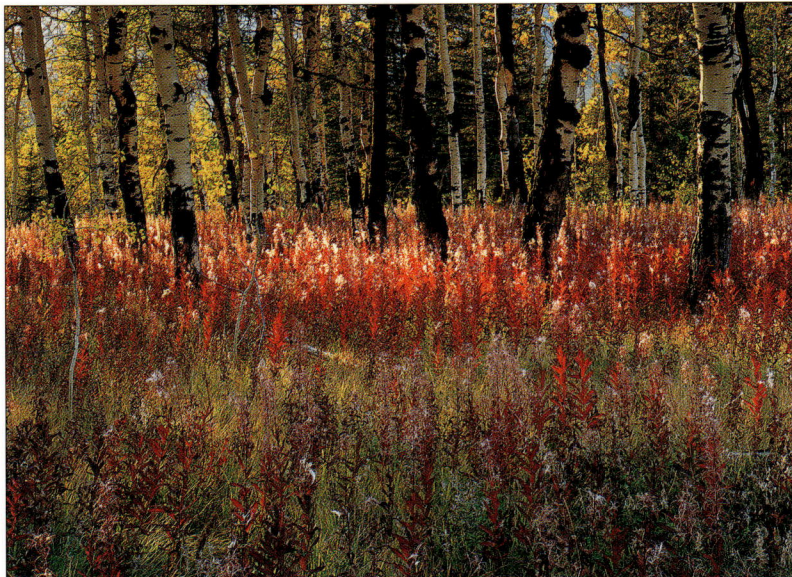

Aspen grove with fireweed, autumn. PHOTO ©LELAND HOWARD

Morning reflections at Leigh Lake. PHOTO ©TIM FITZHARRIS

overlap. The tendency toward a great number and diversity of species in the ecotone is called the "edge effect." Some animals, such as the red squirrel, pine marten, and black bear, spend most of their time in the forests. Others, such as moose, elk, and wolves, seek the forest for shade and shelter during the day and move out to the sagebrush or meadows to feed in the twilight hours.

The loose sedimentary soil of the valley floor holds moisture poorly, resulting in a sparse vegetation cover dominated by sagebrush and coarse grasses. Quaking aspens, cottonwoods, and willows thrive along streams in riparian zones beyond the barren outwash plain. Wet meadows provide the conditions suited to grasses, sedges, and wildflowers. Coyotes and badgers dig burrows in patches of loess, those wind-borne glacial sediments that were blown into the valley between ice ages.

The lower elevations are predominantly treeless, except along watercourses, where cottonwoods and other broad-leaved, deciduous species cluster into riparian habitats and on glacial moraines. Sagebrush steppe communities and grasslands typical of the drier northern plains occur in valleys and basins. Porous valley soils (6,400 – 7,000 feet) support xerophytic plants tolerant of heat and low moisture. In addition to abundant sagebrush, numerous wildflowers and grasses grow. During June and July, a profusion of color enlivens the valley: the yellow of balsamroot, the blue of lupine, and the red of gilia. During August, sunflowers replace balsamroot.

Evergreen forests composed of seven coniferous tree species and more than 900 species of flowering plants dominate the mountainous part of the Teton Range below the tree line and extend into Jackson Hole on top of moraines. Moraines, soil-rich ridges made up of compact piles of unsorted glacial debris, have good clay content, holding moisture better than the quartzite-rich outwash plain. They are thus able to support large stands of lodgepole pine, along with many other plants.

Canyons and subalpine areas lie within elevations of 7,000 – 10,000 feet. Between the crags of the Tetons, Ice Age glaciers have carved deep canyons. Today the canyons contain dense conifer forests and open meadows of wildflowers. As elevation increases, wildflowers abound while trees become stunted and eventually shrublike. Plants often grow very close to the ground, and in the thinning forest near timberline, twisted, contorted, and deformed trees grow. They are called *krummholz,* a German word that means "elfin timber" or "crooked wood."

Alpine areas are characteristic of areas above timberline, 10,000 feet and higher. It is a challenging world, where stocky trees give way upslope and on extremely windy ridges to bare fields (fell fields) with sparse, low-growing vegetation and scattered boulders covered with lichen.

Lichens grow in all of the communities. Lichens are cooperative alliances between fungi and algae. The alga uses sunlight to make sugars as food for itself and the fungus. The fungus provides protection from environmental stressors such as excess light. Lichens are one of the best examples of symbiosis, relationships between species in which there is mutual benefit to both organisms. If lichens growing on a boulder are examined with a hand lens, they look like miniature coral reefs. One scientist has even called them "the forests of Lilliput."

Most of the trees in the park are conifers because of the short growing season. Conifers retain their leaves (needles) throughout the year and can produce food through sunlight (photosynthesis) on warm spring days. Deciduous trees shed their leaves in the fall and must grow new ones each spring before they can photosynthesize. Aspens and cottonwoods have chlorophyll in the bark, and so can photosynthesize before producing leaves.

ANIMALS: LARGE AND SMALL

Grand Teton National Park is located in the heart of the Greater Yellowstone Ecosystem, one of the largest intact temperate zone ecosystems remaining on the planet. This means that many of the animals in the Teton area travel between the two parks and the numerous adjacent national forests. In an ecological sense, the two parks are inseparably linked because of the ambulatory nature of wild animals.

In Grand Teton, you will find everything from tiny finches and calliope hummingbirds to bald eagles and the endangered trumpeter swan. In its lakes and streams there are 16 species of fish. Four species of reptiles and five of amphibians are found here, among them western chorus frog and the Rocky Mountain rubber boa (a harmless relative of the large boa constrictor of the tropics). Sixty-one species of mammals include all of the large North American wild ungulates, as well as others, ranging from the tiny and voracious masked shrew to the legendary grizzly, or "Great Bear."

Predators range in size from grizzly bears, which may weigh 700 pounds, to hoary bats, which weigh only a fraction of an ounce, to black-winged damselflies that feed on mosquitoes. Other predators include red foxes, coyotes, river otters, pine martens, bobcats, bald eagles, ospreys, harlequin ducks, great gray owls, long-tailed weasels, badgers, and the rare wolverine. Gray wolves, past victims of persecution and misguided management and long absent from the region, have recently been successfully restored in Yellowstone but are not seen in Grand Teton.

Sadly, there are species of vertebrates and invertebrates within the park that are listed as rare, threatened, or even endangered. Their demise motivates scientists and resource managers to

Sagebrush one year after a fire near Blacktail Butte. PHOTO ©GEORGE WUERTHNER

Willows at Oxbow Bend on the Snake River. PHOTO ©ALAN MAJCHROWICZ

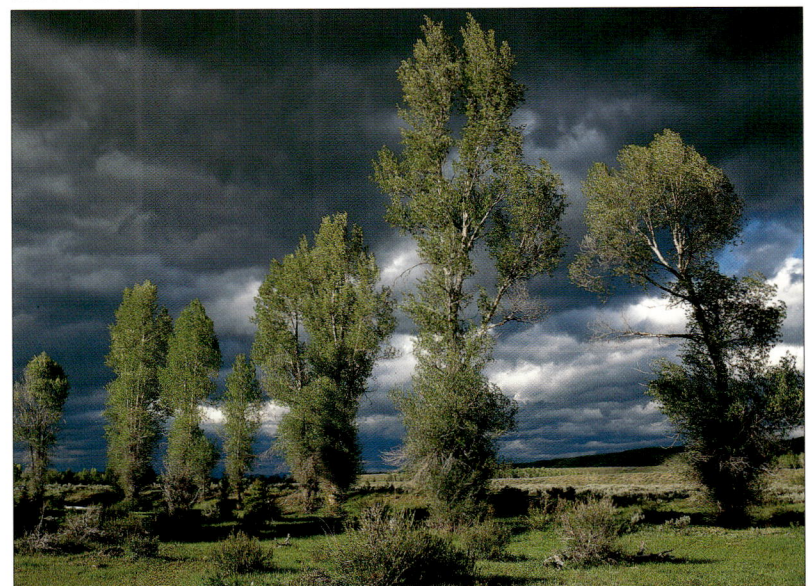

Cottonwoods on the plain near the Gros Ventre River. PHOTO ©JEFF GNASS

Grizzly bear. PHOTO ©HOWIE GARBER/IDAHO STOCK IMAGES

Two elk bulls locking antlers, late autumn. PHOTO ©CAROL POLICH

Mountain lion stalking in the snow. PHOTO ©TIM FITZHARRIS

be vigilant, to continue their study of the connections among animal populations, and to adopt multiple-species management in the context of a larger ecosystem.

The Greater Yellowstone Ecosystem mammal fauna includes one of two remaining large, self-regulating grizzly bear populations in the lower 48 states (the other is in Glacier National Park along the Canadian border). The grizzly's smaller relative, the black bear, is present in larger numbers, but neither species is as frequently seen as in the past. This is not necessarily an indication of decreasing numbers. In recent years, more enlightened wildlife management policies have eliminated artificial feeding, a practice that led to the frequent appearance of bears at roadsides and garbage dumps. Deprived of this often-unhealthy food source, the bears have simply dispersed back into more remote sections of the park, a much healthier situation for bears and people. Grizzlies, several of which have been recently observed, are now well established in the park.

Elk, also known by the Shawnee Indian word *wapiti*, are the most easily and frequently seen large mammals. The elk population level varies with the severity of winter, predation, and range conditions. There are several thousand individuals in different migratory herds of varying size. Altogether, there may be about 90,000 elk throughout the Greater Yellowstone Ecosystem, making it the largest herd in North America.

The North American bison population, thought to have numbered almost 60 million in the 1800s, was reduced so drastically that it was thought that there were fewer than 50 animals by the beginning of the 20th century. The bison was saved from extinction at a ranch in the Lamar Valley of Yellowstone National Park, where its numbers gradually increased. The American bison, the largest terrestrial animal in North America, is commonly but incorrectly called the buffalo, a name more properly applied to the cape buffalo of Africa. Bison are frequently seen throughout the park.

Shiras moose are abundant in the park and often encountered in open meadows and along stream courses. They are large, clumsy-looking animals but surprisingly swift and graceful. Moose are the largest members of the deer family in the world and have massive antlers that look a little like palm fronds.

The mule deer population is large. Mule deer, sometimes called black-tailed deer, summer at higher elevations but move down to warmer, sheltered valleys during the long winters. Mule deer are related to white-tailed deer, which have a characteristic large "flag" tail and are seen occasionally in lower-elevation grass and shrub lands, but mule deer have short, black-tipped tails and very large ears. Deer tend to move down to drink at streams and rivers at dusk. Large herds of them may often be seen in nearby open fields.

Rocky Mountain bighorn sheep are sure-footed rock climbers and jumpers. There are few bighorns in the park. Grand Teton bighorn populations remain in the high country year round. They are distinguished by massive curled horns, especially in males.

Pronghorn are found in lower, drier, sagebrush-steppe and plains environments. Pronghorn look like they were imported from the Serengeti Plain in East Africa. The pronghorn is neither an antelope nor a goat, nor is it even closely related. It is the sole remnant of an ancient ungulate family dating back 20 million years. Pronghorn are capable of running at speeds of 70 miles an hour. They can leap nearly 30 feet in a single bound; yet they cannot jump fences like deer.

Mountain lions, bobcats, and lynx occur in the park. Beaver are abundant in aquatic settings, and there are variable numbers of foxes, badgers, river otters, weasels, martens, and other small mammals. Wolverines are known to exist but they are only rarely sighted in Grand Teton.

Visitors tend to be focused on sighting the large and spectacular mammals, often dubbed "charismatic megafauna." But there are smaller mammals, some seldom seen, that play important roles in the natural processes of the larger ecosystem. In numbers they far exceed their showier, more charismatic, relatives. Many of them are so small and secretive that they are seldom seen. Sometimes their trails, burrows, or nests are the only evidence of their presence. Still, they are key to the survival of the larger critters. A coyote may feed on red-backed voles, northern pocket gophers, snowshoe hares, Uinta ground squirrels, deer mice, frogs, toads, and occasional birds. White bark pine seeds, harvested by red squirrels and Clark's nutcrackers and cached in middens throughout the forest, are later visited by grizzly bears emerging from hibernation.

Birds represent the greatest species diversity among vertebrates in Grand Teton, including species that are known to nest in the region, or that are passing through, on their way to different locations. Most birds found in the park migrate to lower elevations and more southern latitudes starting in September.

Biologists are carefully monitoring the status of several bird species, including bald eagles, American white pelicans, common loons, harlequin ducks, great gray owls, and various colonial nesting birds. Researchers believe that the regional population of the trumpeter swan, the largest wildfowl in North America, is recovering from earlier lows.

A great variety of warblers, wrens, finches, sparrows, blackbirds, tanagers, buntings, and other perching birds add sound and color to the air. Various ducks, geese, grebes, herons, American dippers, belted kingfishers, and other water-loving birds

Bull moose at Willow Flats. PHOTO ©CAROL POLICH

Badger. PHOTO ©TIM FITZHARRIS

Beaver gnawing on aspen branch. PHOTO ©DIANA STRATTON

Trumpeter swan.

are attracted to the many aquatic habitats in Grand Teton. The dipper, once known as the water ouzel, is always found near rapids and fast-moving water. In deeper areas, it dives into the water and runs along the bottom with half-open wings, searching for aquatic insects.

Near the bottom of many food chains are copepods (small crustaceans) and other zooplankton living in Grand Teton's waters, as well as millions of insects. Insects are responsible for the greatest diversity among park invertebrates. Thousands of species of insects, ranging from aphids to wasps, have been observed.

Reptiles and amphibians are also present in the park, although in small numbers. Cold blooded, they have to absorb much of their body heat from the environment in which they live. The long cold winters and the overall dry conditions of the park limit their population to only five known amphibians and four reptile species.

Wildlife populations tend toward a state of dynamic equilibrium with the physical environment and its plant communities. Park managers make science-based decisions that favor natural population regulation through predation, harsh winters, changing range conditions, and other factors. Human intervention in natural processes is limited and tends only to happen when visitor safety is an issue, such as when a bear that has repeatedly placed campers in jeopardy is relocated or euthanized, as a last resort. Habitat fragmentation by development of visitor use facilities is minimized. In Grand Teton, people are visitors in the house that Nature built. Wildlife has a prior right to this place.

The Sum of The Parts: A Greater Ecosystem

Spectacular fall color along Palisades Creek, Targhee National Forest.
PHOTO ©LELAND HOWARD

All ecosystems, from a miniature community of lichens growing on a few square inches of rock to an area that includes entire mountain ranges, have edges. But, their edges are not straight and angular. Rather, like living organisms, they are soft and contoured.

Animals and plants neither see nor respect the boundaries that people have drawn, and lines on a map do not deter natural processes. Acknowledging these ecological truths, scientists and resource managers have increasingly looked beyond the conventional legal boundaries of parks for relationships and connections. Using Yellowstone National Park as a central element, scientists have defined a Greater Yellowstone Ecosystem—a description that aptly conveys a sense of both the remarkable size and the great significance of the area (see map on page 59).

With the exception of the Alaskan wilderness, the Greater Yellowstone Ecosystem may be the largest, biologically richest and most complex ecosystem in North America. Greater numbers and varieties of animal species live in the larger Yellowstone region than any other place in the coterminous United States

The Greater Yellowstone Ecosystem is an aggregation of countless smaller systems. Each is discrete and essentially self-sustaining, yet all are connected through the intricate and precisely ordered mechanisms of ecological processes. The greater ecosystem represents the whole organism, not just one of its organs. It is an affirmation that, ecologically, the whole is greater than the sum of its parts. It is the larger context of life and environment in which each smaller system operates, and upon which they rely for their health and vitality.

Plants produce the food that sustains the animal life of the Greater Yellowstone Ecosystem by capturing solar energy through photosynthesis and absorbing nutrients from the soil and water.

Photosynthesized food is passed from herbivores (plant eaters) to carnivores (meat eaters), which are in turn consumed by larger carnivores. Grass becomes flesh and bone; the mosquito becomes the damselfly; the damselfly becomes the trout; the trout becomes the bear. The sequence in which energy and nutrients pass from producers through successive levels of consumers is known as a food chain, and each stage in the transfer of energy is called a trophic level. Food chains combine into larger more complex patterns called food webs.

Living matter is consumed in grazing food chains. Dead matter is consumed in detrital food chains. Some microbes are part of food chains that consume dissolved organic matter. A typical grazing food chain in Grand Teton could include algae that form the diet of mosquito larvae. The mosquito larvae in turn become lunch for a trout. The trout then becomes a meal for a pelican, otter, bear, or a hungry angler.

Detrital food chains are most common in natural systems where less than 10 percent of the green plants that are the mainstay of that ecosystem are grazed. In such a system, substantial and complex buildups of biomass, the total weight of living matter in a given area, can occur, increasing energy storage in the system. A typical detrital food chain in Grand Teton could begin with dead plant material eaten by bacteria and fungi, which are then consumed by single-celled animals. Worms and insects eat the protozoans, and are in turn consumed by birds.

The relationship of numbers and size of organisms in a food chain is inverted and depicted graphically as a pyramid of numbers. From bottom to top of the pyramid, the numbers decrease and the size of the organisms increases. The greatest amount of energy available is in the green plants, the primary producers, at

OPPOSITE: Aerial view of the Tetons and Alaska Basin from the southwest.
PHOTO ©MICHAEL COLLIER

Gray wolves roaming in Yellowstone National Park. PHOTO ©TIM FITZHARRIS

Bison in Lamar Valley, Yellowstone National Park. PHOTO ©TIM FITZHARRIS

Bull elks bugling, early morning. PHOTO ©TIM FITZHARRIS

the base of the pyramid, with successive levels of consumers (primary, secondary, tertiary) above them. The higher the organism is on the trophic pyramid, the less energy is available to it.

Solar heat and light flow through and energize the entire system, except in the dark throats of geysers and hot springs. In nearly every functioning ecosystem the ultimate source of energy is the sun. Self-nourishing organisms, known as autotrophs or producers, convert and concentrate the solar energy into food. Consumers, or heterotrophs, are animals and plants such as bladderworts that utilize, rearrange, and decompose material made by the producers. Decomposers are the link between death and new life.

The primary energy source for consumers is food, a direct or indirect product of photosynthesis. Based on whether they are plant eaters, meat eaters, both, or decomposers, consumers are designated as herbivores (elk, deer, bison, and other ungulates); carnivores (wolves, bobcats, mountain lions); omnivores (grizzly bears, black bears, people); or saprovores (microorganisms that consume dead and dying organisms such as slime molds and bacteria),

Ecological systems import and export energy and materials across the conventional boundaries on maps, and the integrity of both the individual ecosystem and adjacent areas is dependent on those exchanges, or ecological subsidies. Within the system, connections are made on many pathways—the air and soil, wildlife ranges and immigration and migration routes, surface streams and subterranean aquifers, ridges and valleys, roads and trails.

Nutrients, elements, and inorganic compounds that are essential to life are circulated through the Greater Yellowstone Ecosystem in what are called material cycles. The hydrologic cycle is perhaps the best known. It involves the perpetual circulation of water through evapotranspiration, the combination of evaporation and transpiration, or water loss from plants, condensation, and precipitation. In addition to the water cycle, others that circulate nitrogen, phosphorous, sulfur, and carbon through the system are important.

One of the best ways to visualize and understand these interrelationships is to think of the ecosystem as a living organism. Air and water are its metaphoric breath and blood; carbon, nitrogen, phosphorous, and other compounds are its foods. If not properly balanced, they can cause illness. Green plants and air-breathing animals, including people, are the lungs of the ecosystem. The sun energizes the movement of air, water, and nutrients through the ecosystem. Energy is transferred in the larger area and its lifeforms, through various ecological relationships that connect everything, like arteries and veins in a complex circulatory system.

The wisdom of considering Grand Teton and Yellowstone unbounded by political lines is confirmed by our understanding of ecosystem functioning and animal behavior. A mature grizzly bear can range over 1,000 square miles in a single season. The migratory routes of elk and bison place them well beyond the park. The seasonal migration of the pronghorn requires a range of more than 200 miles, from the Grand Teton high country south to the Red Desert. Wildland fires (such as those of 1988) move freely, and capriciously, across legal boundaries.

Some ecologists have suggested that, as formerly continuous natural habitats (ecosystems) are increasingly fragmented by the encroachment of civilization, they begin to develop the characteristics of remote islands and archipelagoes. Parks like Grand Teton have been likened to land-bridge islands because most of them are slowly becoming isolated from their surroundings by habitat disturbances beyond their boundaries, and in effect, are as ecologically isolated as true islands.

In a sense, Grand Teton, and places like it, are analogs to the "commons" of 19th-century England. The concept of the commons recognized that there are some pieces of land, or elements of the environment, that never have been and should never be held in private ownership. Unfortunately, many such places suffer what has been called the "tragedy of the commons," as they are shared, used, misused, and sometimes abused by increasing numbers of common owners. Often there is little sense of common cause for the common property. Sometimes, too, lines on a map delineate adjacent areas in which inappropriate uses or differing management philosophies prevail. Large ecosystems can become disarticulated because common management is not always a companion of common use.

Unlike some large ecosystems, such as the Everglades in Florida, the greater Yellowstone system has not suffered the rapid acceleration of natural change that results from extensive human manipulation. It has remained an essentially pristine vignette of primitive North America. Still, there are persistent threats to its integrity as a wild system, in spite of its relative remoteness. Among the problems are habitat loss and fragmentation, human population growth, deterioration of air and water quality, proliferation of exotic species, increasing physical developments, and differing policies of resource management agencies within the system. Habitat fragmentation is a particularly insidious threat to species approaching the one-way-road to extinction. It is like randomly removing pieces from a completed jigsaw puzzle across which those animals must move to survive.

Ecologists speak of a cumulative-effects model. They know that in any ecosystem, manipulations of species or their environments seldom have singular effects. Rather, the effects of one

Red-tailed hawk and prey. PHOTO ©TIM FITZHARRIS

Pronghorn portrait. PHOTO ©TIM FITZHARRIS

Grain elevator and the Tetons seen from near Drummond, Idaho, sunset.

change, however small, tend to magnify many times over as they spread through the ecosystem like ripples moving outward from a stone tossed on the surface of a lake.

The Greater Yellowstone Coalition was formed in 1983 to help promote the concept of a greater ecosystem and defend its health and survival. Since then, the coalition has fought to ensure that resource management is not done in a fragmented manner but, instead, in a coordinated fashion considering the entire ecosystem. With the help of federal, state, and local agencies and the work of thousands of volunteers, this organization has managed to define and promote the concept of ecosystem management with great success.

Using the application of science, common sense, and greater cooperation among all involved, the Greater Yellowstone Coalition lobbies for the protection of Yellowstone, its greater ecosystem and all its resources, while promoting sustainable growth and quality of life for human beings who are also part of the ecosystem. In managing large ecosystems, our concerns must reach beyond the boundaries that conventionally define those systems. Ecosystem management must also be applied to areas beyond, or geographically isolated from, the perimeter of the Greater Yellowstone Ecosystem.

One effort looks far beyond the boundaries of the Greater Yellowstone Ecosystem. The Yellowstone to Yukon Conservation Initiative is a joint Canadian and United States network of more than 340 organizations (including the Greater Yellowstone Coalition), institutions, foundations, and many conservation-minded individuals who have recognized the value of working together to restore and maintain the unique natural heritage of the Yellowstone to Yukon region and the quality of life it offers. One of its concerns is the preservation of corridors for wildlife movement among disarticulated habitats.

At 2.2 million acres and situated to the north of Grand Teton, Yellowstone National Park is the core of the larger Greater Yellowstone Ecosystem. The larger ecosystem covers nearly 18 million acres in northwest Wyoming, southwest Montana, and southeast Idaho, and includes six national forests, three national wildlife refuges, and lands managed by the Bureau of Land Management. Altogether, federal lands total 13.9 million acres. In addition, there are 500,000 acres of state land in Wyoming, Montana, and Idaho, including land on three Indian reservations and about 3.3 million acres of private inholdings within the ecosystem.

As part of the Greater Yellowstone Ecosystem, Grand Teton and Jackson Hole are in the heart of a complex of scenic natural areas. Gallatin National Forest, established in 1899, borders Yellowstone National Park on the north and northwest. More than 40 percent of the forest is designated roadless wilderness, including the Absaroka-Beartooth Wilderness. Shoshone National Forest, the first national forest in the United States, adjoins Yellowstone along most of its eastern boundary. It was established in 1891 as part of the Yellowstone Timberland Reserve. Shoshone National Forest includes the North Absaroka Wilderness and portions of the Beartooth Plateau and Absaroka, Beartooth, and Wind River ranges. Custer National Forest forms part of the northeast quadrant of the greater ecosystem. Bridger-Teton National Forest, originally established in 1897 as the Teton Forest Preserve, wraps around the southern edge of Yellowstone National Park and the eastern and southern margins of Grand Teton. It comprises a substantial part of the larger ecosystem and includes the vast Teton Wilderness. Caribou-Targhee National Forest adjoins Grand Teton on its western boundary and touches Yellowstone along its southwest margin. The Beaverhead-Deerlodge National Forest lies in the northwest part of the Greater Yellowstone Ecosystem.

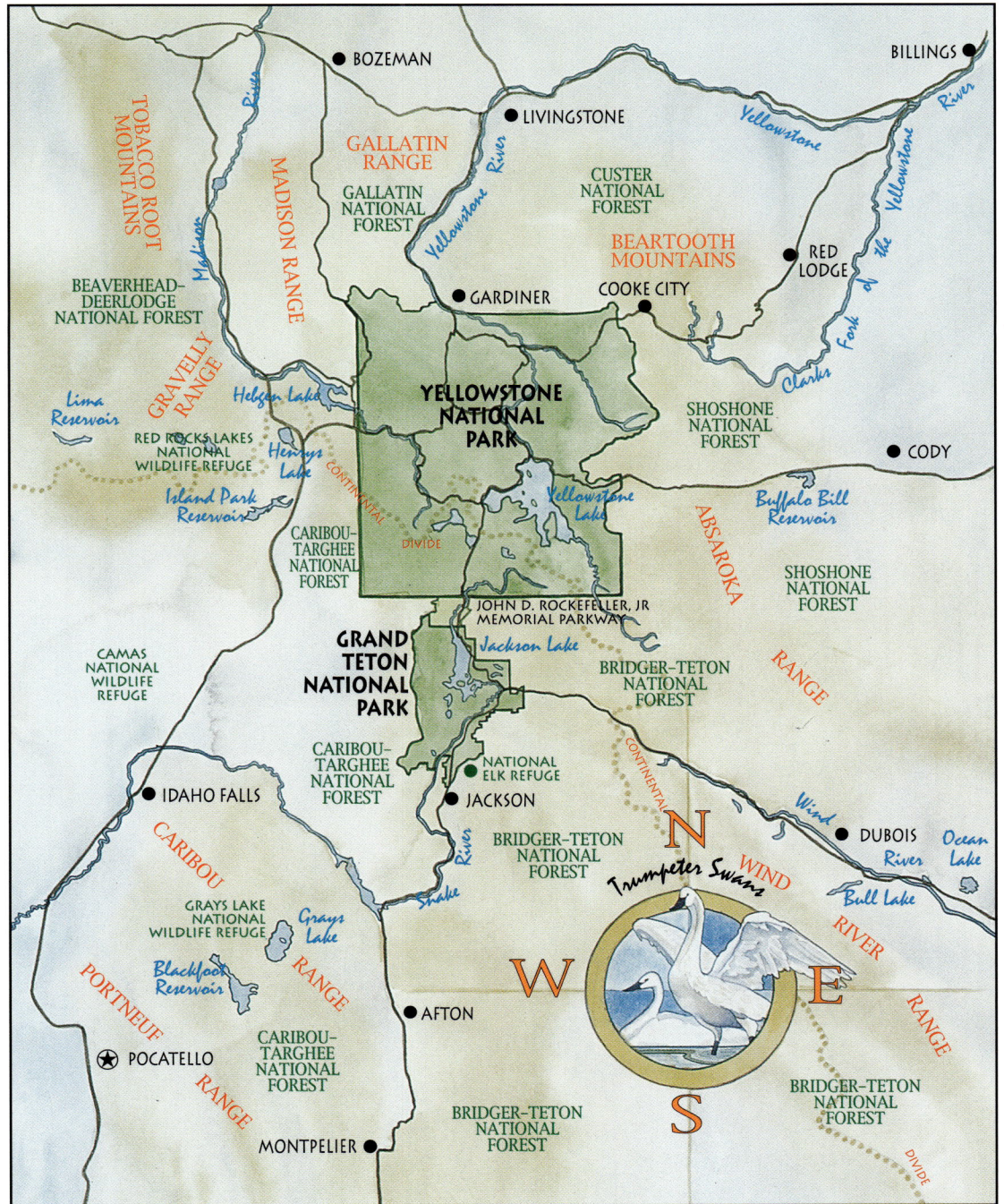

Three important wildlife refuges are located nearby. Grays Lake National Wildlife Refuge, the largest hard-stem bulrush marsh in North America, is located in a high mountain valley near Soda Springs in southeastern Idaho. The refuge hosts a large nesting population of greater sandhill cranes. Red Rocks Lakes National Wildlife Refuge, in the rugged Centennial Mountains, focuses on restoring declining populations of the majestic trumpeter swan. The National Elk Refuge provides winter habitat for the nationally significant Jackson elk herd.

"...I realized that, in spite of the closeness of civilization and the changes that hemmed it in, this remnant of the old wilderness would speak to me of silence and solitude, of belonging and wonder and beauty."

—Sigurd Olson

ILLUSTRATION BY DARLECE CLEVELAND

PAGE 60/61: Sunrise at Schwabacher Landing. PHOTO ©TIM FITZHARRIS

IN CASE OF EMERGENCY

Emergency & Medical
   Call 911
   —or—
Grand Teton National Park
   (307) 739-3301 (Emergencies Only)

INFORMATION

Current Road Conditions
(307) 739-3682

Grand Teton National Park
PO Drawer 170
Moose, WY 83012
(307) 739-3399
www.nps.gov/grte

Grand Teton
Natural History Association
PO Box 170
Moose, WY 83012
(307) 739-3606
www.grandtetonpark.org

Grand Teton
National Park Foundation
PO Box 249
Moose, WY 83012
(307) 732-0629
www.gtnpf.org

Teton Science School
PO Box 68
Kelly, WY 83011
(307) 733-4765

VISITOR CENTERS

Colter Bay Visitor Center and
Indian Arts Museum
Open mid–May to early–October
(307) 739-3594

Flagg Ranch Information Station
Open early–June to early–September
(307) 543-2372

Jenny Lake Visitor Center
Open mid–May to late–September
(307) 739-3392

Craig Thomas Discovery and
Visitor Center
Open year round.
(307) 739-3399

Laurance S. Rockefeller Preserve
Open June to mid–September

PARK LODGING

Colter Bay Village and Cabins
(800) 628-9988
www.gtlc.com

Dornan's Spur Ranch Log Cabins
PO Box 39
Moose, WY 83012
(307) 733-2522
www.dornans.com

Flagg Ranch
PO Box 187
Moran, WY 83013
(800) 443-2311
www.flaggranch.com

Jackson Lake Lodge
PO Box 250
Moran, WY 83013
(800) 628-9988
www.gtlc.com

Jenny Lake Lodge
PO Box 240
Moran, WY 83013
(800) 628-9988
www.gtlc.com

Luton's Teton Cabins
PO Box 48
Moran, WY 83013
(307) 543-2489

Signal Mountain Lodge
PO Box 50
Moran, WY 83013
(307) 543-2831
http://foreverlodging.com

Togwotee Mountain Lodge
PO Box 91
Moran, WY 83013
(307) 543-2847
www.togwoteelodge.com

LODGING OUTSIDE THE PARK

Jackson Hole
Chamber of Commerce
990 W. Broadway/PO Box 550
Jackson, WY 83001
(307) 733-3316

PARK CAMPING

Colter Bay Campground
Open mid–May to late–September
(800) 628-9988

Flagg Ranch Campground
Open late–May to late–September
(800) 443-2311

Gros Ventre Campground
Open early–May to mid–October
(800) 628-9988

Jenny Lake Campground
Open mid–May to late–September
(800) 628-9988

Lizard Creek Campground
Open early–June to early–September
(800) 672-6012

Signal Mountain Campground
Open mid–May to mid–October
(800) 672-6012

Wilderness Permits
Grand Teton National Park
Permits Office, PO Drawer 170
Moose, WY 83012
(307) 739-3309 or 739-3397 for
information only. No reservations accepted by phone.
www.nps.gov/grte/planyourvisit/bcres.htm.

OTHER REGIONAL SITES

Bighorn Canyon NRA
PO Box 7458
Fort Smith, MT 59035
(406) 666-2412
www.nps.gov/bica

Big Hole National Battlefield
PO Box 237
Wisdom, MT 59761
(406) 689-3155
www.nps.gov/biho

ABOVE: Summer sunset at Colter Bay, Jackson Lake. PHOTO ©JEFF GNASS

City of Rocks National Reserve
PO Box 169
Almo, ID 83312
(208) 824-5519
www.nps.gov/ciro

**Craters of The Moon
National Monument and Preserve**
PO Box 29
Arco, ID 83213
(208) 527-3257
www.nps.gov/crmo
    and/or
Bureau of Land Management Field
Office
(208) 732-7200

Devils Tower National Monument
PO Box 10
Devils Tower, WY 82714
(307) 467-5283
www.nps.gov/deto

Fossil Butte National Monument
PO Box 592
Kemmerer, WY 83101
(307) 877-4455
www.nps.gov/fobu

Glacier National Park
PO Box 128
West Glacier, MT 59936
(406) 888-7800
www.nps.gov/glac

**Grant–Kohrs Ranch
National Historic Site**
266 Warren Lane
Deer Lodge, MT 59722
(406) 846-2070x250
www.nps.gov/grko

**Hagerman Fossil Beds
National Monument**
PO box 570
Hagerman, ID 83332
(208) 837-4793x5227
www.nps.gpv/hafo

**Little Bighorn Battlefield
National Monument**
PO Box 39
Crow Agency, MT 59022
(406) 638-3204
www.nps.gov/libi

John D. Rockefeller, Jr. Memorial Parkway
c/o Grand Teton National Park
PO Drawer 170
Moose, WY 83012
(307) 739-3300
www.nps.gov/grte

Yellowstone National Park
PO Box 168
Yellowstone National Park, WY 82190
(307) 344-7381
www.nps.gov/yell

NATIONAL FOREST INFORMATION

Beaverhead–Deerlodge National Forest
420 Barrett Street
Dillon, MT 59725
(406) 683-3900 or (406) 683-3913
www.fs.fed.us/r1/b-d
Additional District Offices in:

Wise River, MT; Wisdom, MT; Butte, MT; Whitehall, MT; Philipsburg, MT; Deer Lodge, MT; Ennis, MT; and Sheridan, MT.

Bridger–Teton National Forest
PO Box 1888
Jackson, WY 83001
(307) 739-5500
www.fs.fed.us/r4/btnf
Additional District Offices in:
Demmerer, WY; Afton, WY; Moran, WY; Big Piney, WY; and Pinedale, WY.

Caribou–Targhee National Forest
1405 Hollipark Drive
Idaho Falls, ID 83401
(208) 524-7500
www.fs.fed.us/r4/caribou-targhee

Additonal District Offices in:
Ashton, ID; Island Park, ID; Dubois, ID; Montpelier, ID; Soda Springs, ID; Driggs, ID; Pocatello, ID; and Malad, ID.

Custer National Forest
1310 Main Street
Billings, MT 59105
(406) 657-6200

www.fs.fed.us/r1/custer
Additional District Offices in:
Ashland, MT; Camp Crook, SD; and Red Lodge, MT

Gallatin National Forest
PO Box 130
Bozeman, MT 59771
(406) 587-6701
www.fs.fed.us/r1/gallatin
Additional District Offices in:
Big Timber, MT; Livingston, MT; Garkiner, MT; Bozeman, MT; and West Yellowstone, MT.

Shoshone National Forest
808 Meadow Lane
Cody, MT 82414
(307) 527-6241
www.fs.fed.us/r2/shoshone

NATIONAL WILDLIFE REFUGE INFORMATION

Grays Lake NWR
74 Grays Lake road
Wayan, ID 83285
(208) 574-2755
www.fws.gov/grayslake

National Elk Refuge
PO Box 510
Jackson, WY 83002
(307) 733-9212
www.fws.gov/nationalelkrefuge

Red Rock NWR
27820 Southside Centennial Road
Lima, MT 59739
(406) 276-3536
www.fws.gov/redrocks/rr11

**Snake River Birds of Prey
National Conservation Area**
Bureau of Land Management
Four Rivers Field Office
3948 Development Avenue
Boise, ID 83705
(208) 384-3300
www.birdsofprey.blm.gov/

PRODUCTION CREDITS

Publisher: Jeff D. Nicholas
Author: George B. Robinson
Editor: Nicky Leach
Illustrations: Darlece Cleveland
Printing Coordination: Sung In Printing America

ISBN 13: 978-1-58071-075-6
ISBN 10: 1-58071-075-1
©2008 Panorama International Productions, Inc.

SIERRA PRESS
4988 Gold Leaf Drive, Mariposa, CA 95338
(209) 966-5071, 966-5073 (Fax)

Visit our Website:
www.NationalParksUSA.com

OPPOSITE
Dramatic sunset over Jackson Lake from Signal Mountain Overlook.
PHOTO ©JOSHUA HENSON/IDAHO STOCK IMAGES

BELOW
Mule deer buck, autumn. PHOTO ©STAN OSOLINSKI